pilgrim

THE EUCHARIST
A COURSE FOR THE CHRISTIAN JOURNEY

Church Publishing
NEW YORK

Authors and Contributors

Authors

Stephen Cottrell is the Bishop of Chelmsford
Steven Croft is the Bishop of Sheffield
Paula Gooder is a leading New Testament writer and lecturer
Robert Atwell is the Bishop of Exeter
Sharon Ely Pearson is a Christian educator in The Episcopal Church

Contributors

Simon Jones is the Chaplain of Merton College Oxford
Angela Tilby is a Canon of Christ Church Oxford and Continuing Ministerial Development Adviser for the Diocese of Oxford
John Inge is the Bishop of Worcester
John Pritchard is the Bishop of Oxford

pilgrim

THE EUCHARIST
A COURSE FOR THE CHRISTIAN JOURNEY

STEPHEN COTTRELL
STEVEN CROFT
PAULA GOODER
ROBERT ATWELL
SHARON ELY PEARSON

Contributions from
ANGELA TILBY   SIMON JONES
JOHN PRITCHARD   JOHN INGE

Church Publishing
NEW YORK

Cover image—Bread image: Syrota Vadym/Shutterstock.com
Under license from Shutterstock.com

ISBN-13: 978-0-89869-958-6 (pbk.)
ISBN-13: 978-0-89869-959-3 (ebook)

First published in the United Kingdom in 2014 by

Church House Publishing
Church House
Great Smith Street
London SW1P 3AZ

First published in the United States in 2016 by

Church Publishing, Incorporated.
19 East 34th Street
New York, New York 10016
www.churchpublishing.org

Cover and contents design by David McNeill, Revo Design.

Library of Congress Cataloging-in-Publication data

A record of this book is available from the Library of Congress.

Printed in the United States of America

CONTENTS

Welcome to Pilgrim   vi

Introduction to The Eucharist   1

Session One: Your Ancestors Ate Manna in the Wilderness   5

Session Two: This Is My Body Broken for You   15

Session Three: He Was Made Known to Them in the Breaking of
the Bread   23

Session Four: If You Hear My Voice and Open the Door, I Will
Come in and Eat with You   33

Session Five: Do This to Remember Me   41

Session Six: I Am the Bread of Life   49

Notes   58

WELCOME TO *PILGRIM*

Welcome to this course of exploration into the truth of the Christian faith as it has been revealed in Jesus Christ and lived out in the Church down through the centuries.

The aim of this course is to help people explore what it means to be disciples of Jesus Christ. From the very beginning of his ministry, Jesus called people to follow him and become his disciples. The first disciples were called to be with Jesus and to be sent out (Mark 3:14). The Church in every generation shares in the task of helping others hear Christ's call to follow him and to live in his service.

The *Pilgrim* material consists of two groups of four short courses. The **Follow** stage is designed for those who are beginning to explore the faith and what following Jesus will mean. It focuses on four great texts which have been particularly significant to Christian people from the earliest days of the Church:

● The Baptismal Covenant (drawn from the Creeds)

● The Lord's Prayer

● The Beatitudes

● The Commandments

The Follow stage is a beginning in the Christian journey. There is much still to be learned. The four courses in the **Grow** stage—of which this is one—aim to take you further and deeper, building on the Follow stage. They focus on:

● The Creeds

● The Eucharist (and the whole life of prayer and worship)

- The Bible
- The Church and the kingdom (living your whole life as a disciple)

We hope that, in the Grow stage, people will learn the essentials for a life of discipleship. We hope that you will do this in the company of a small group of fellow travelers: people like you who want to find out more about the Christian faith and are considering its claims and challenges.

The material in the Grow stage can also be used by people who have been Christians for many years as a way of deepening their discipleship.

We have designed the material in the Grow stage so that it can be led by the members of the group: you don't need an expert or a teacher to guide you through. *Pilgrim* aims to help you learn by encouraging you to practice the ancient disciplines of biblical reflection and prayer which have always been at the heart of the living out of Christian faith.

The format is similar to the Follow stage. Each book has six sessions and, in each session, you will find:

- a **theme**
- some **opening prayers**
- a "**conversation-starter**"
- an opportunity to reflect on a **reading** from Scripture (the Bible)
- a short **reflection** on the theme from a contemporary Christian writer
- **some questions** to address together
- a "**journeying on**" section
- some **closing prayers**
- finally, there are selected quotations from the great tradition of Christian writing to aid further reflection.

You will find a greater emphasis in the Grow stage on learning to tell the story of God's work in your life to others as every disciple is called to be a witness. You will also find a greater emphasis on learning to live out your faith in everyday life. The Journeying On section includes an individual challenge for the week ahead and you are encouraged to share your progress as part of the Conversation as you meet for the next session.

INTRODUCTION TO *THE EUCHARIST*

Many years ago, I visited Mother Teresa's home for the destitute in Calcutta. As the sick and dying were brought in off the streets, they were laid on beds in cubicles where sisters washed their bodies and tended their sores. Above each bed was a sign in English fixed to the wall which said, "The Body of Christ." There is a link between our sharing in the Eucharist, our calling to be Christ's body in the world, and our service to others. As Jesus says in the parable of the sheep and goats, "Just as you did it to the least of my brothers and sisters, you did it to me" (Matthew 25:40). To put it crudely, if we can't recognize the presence of Christ in the destitute and dying, we are unlikely to recognize him in the breaking of the bread.

Historians tell us that the oldest religious ritual continuously observed in the world is Passover, when each year Jews commemorate their escape from slavery in Egypt. Like the Passover, the Eucharist is anchored in history and is celebrated by Christians the world over as a memorial of Christ's saving passion and resurrection. "Do this in remembrance of me," says Jesus, and for 2,000 years Christians have faithfully obeyed his command. It is why the Eucharist stands at the heart of Christian worship.

We do not know for certain whether or not the Last Supper Jesus held with his disciples on the night he was betrayed was a Passover meal, but it is likely. Throughout his ministry Jesus certainly had special fellowship meals with his disciples and he had the habit of breaking bread and sharing it. It was this characteristic action that opened the eyes of two disciples to his identity at Emmaus after his resurrection. At the Last Supper in the Upper Room, as Jesus broke the bread and gave thanks (for the wine), he associated these things with his own imminent death and thereby gave to them a spiritual significance that continues to shape the Christian community.

Christians celebrate this action in a variety of contexts and in a variety of ways. Like all meals it can be anything from a banquet, complete with exquisite music and ceremony, to a picnic where the emphasis is on simplicity and informality. The titles that Christians give to the service also vary. Some refer to it as the **Lord's Supper**, emphasizing the fact that at heart this is a sacred meal. Episcopalians tend to call it either **Holy Communion** or the **Eucharist**.

The title **Holy Communion** reminds us that we are not observers but participants, guests at the Lord's Table, where God feeds us spiritually with his body and blood. The title **Eucharist**, meaning thanksgiving, is an ancient one as the Greek origin of the word implies. We give thanks for all that God has given us in Christ. This is summed up in the great Prayer of Thanksgiving or Eucharistic Prayer that the priest presiding at the service prays in the name of all assembled. The title **Mass**, commonly used by Roman Catholics, derives from the Latin of the closing words of the service, "Go in peace to love and serve the Lord." We gather around God's table to remember Christ's sacrifice before being sent out as a "living sacrifice" to live and work to God's praise and glory. Whatever title is used, it is the same God who invites us to the table as a foretaste of the heavenly banquet prepared for all people.

There is nothing automatic about this sacramental meal, this "outward and visible sign" of God's abundant grace. It is why Episcopalians hesitate to define *how* God is present. As the poet John Donne famously wrote, "He was the Word that spake it; he took the bread and brake it; and what that Word did make it, I do believe and take it."[1] Augustine went as far as to suggest that it is the sacrament of ourselves that is placed on the Lord's Table and which we receive. "Be then," he says, "a member of Christ's body so that your Amen may accord with the truth."[2] As we worship together we grow into becoming who we are meant to be: the Body of Christ.

Celebrating the hospitality of God, praising God for all that God has done for us in Christ, communing with our risen Lord, and being renewed in our service of others are all aspects of the Eucharist that we will explore in this course, mindful of Paul's words that every time we break this bread and drink the cup we "proclaim the Lord's death until he comes" (1 Corinthians 11:26).

Since much of the text for this part of *Pilgrim* can be found in the 1979 Book of Common Prayer that is used in your local congregation, we encourage you to obtain a copy and refer to it as you participate in each of these sessions. There is one prayer in particular worth holding onto found on page 366. The congregation often says this post-communion prayer together after everyone has received communion. It offers thanks that God has fed us with the body and blood of Jesus; and we remember that the word Eucharist means "thanksgiving." It reminds us that we must offer our souls and bodies—our whole selves—as a living sacrifice to God (Romans 12:1-2). All worship, whatever the particular service, is about this offering of us. It says that we must be sent out to live and work to God's praise and glory. There is a rhythm to Christian worship: we are gathered in, and we are sent out. Holy Communion is rations for the journey of life. It is also a foretaste of the banquet of heaven.

ROBERT ATWELL

Almighty and everliving God,
we thank you for feeding us with the spiritual food
of the most precious Body and Blood
of your Son our Savior Jesus Christ;
and for assuring us in these holy mysteries
that we are living members of the Body of your Son,
and heirs of your eternal kingdom.
And now, Father, send us out
to do the work you have given us to do,
to love and serve you
as faithful witnesses of Christ our Lord.
To him, to you, and to the Holy Spirit,
be honor and glory, now and for ever. Amen.

YOUR ANCESTORS ATE MANNA IN THE WILDERNESS

pilgrim

In this session we look at worship as communion with God.

Opening Prayers

I am the bread of life,
anyone who comes to me shall not hunger,
anyone who believes in me shall never thirst.
Alleluia. Lord, give us this bread always.

The bread of God comes down from heaven,
and gives life to the world.
Alleluia. Lord, give us this bread always.

Anyone who eats my flesh and drinks my blood has eternal life,
And I will raise them up on the last day.
Alleluia. Lord, give us this bread always.

It is the spirit that gives life; the flesh is of no avail.
The words I speak, they are spirit and they are life.
Alleluia. Lord, give us this bread always.

Walk with us, Lord,
Along the road of resurrection!
Explain for us, so slow to believe,
the things that scripture says of you.
Break the bread of the Eucharist with us
whenever we share our lives with our brothers and sisters.
Stay with us each time night approaches
and the daylight fades in our hearts.
Amen.

Conversation

If someone stopped you in the street and asked, why do you worship, what is it for, how would you reply? What have been your best and most moving experiences of worship?

Reflecting on Scripture

Reading

Jesus said, "I am the bread of life. [49]Your ancestors ate the manna in the wilderness, and they died. [50]This is the bread that comes down from heaven, so that one may eat of it and not die. [51]I am the living bread that came down from heaven. Whoever eats of this bread will live for ever; and the bread that I will give for the life of the world is my flesh."
[52]The Jews then disputed among themselves, saying, "How can this man give us his flesh to eat?" [53]So Jesus said to them, "Very truly, I tell you, unless you eat the flesh of the Son of Man and drink his blood, you have no life in you. [54]Those who eat my flesh and drink my blood have eternal life, and I will raise them up on the last day; [55]for my flesh is true food and my blood is true drink. [56]Those who eat my flesh and drink my blood abide in me, and I in them. [57]Just as the living Father sent me, and I live because of the Father, so whoever eats me will live because of me. [58]This is the bread that came down from heaven, not like that which your ancestors ate, and they died. But the one who eats this bread will live for ever."

JOHN 6:48-58

Explanatory note
In this passage Jesus is referring to the story in Exodus 16:1-36, in which God's people, having just escaped from slavery in Egypt, found themselves in the desert with no food. God miraculously fed them with quail and with a pale, flaky substance that they called manna (the word means literally "what now?").

- Read the passage through once.
- Keep a few moments' silence.
- Read the passage a second time with different voices.
- Invite everyone to say aloud a word or phrase that strikes them.

- Read the passage a third time.
- Share together what this word or phrase might mean and what questions it raises.

Reflection STEPHEN COTTRELL

When I was a stranger you welcomed me

One of the most basic, but often overlooked, symbols of the Christian faith is a table. Think of almost any church you have been into and you will find one. Sometimes it is very grand, high and lifted up and bedecked with candles; sometimes it is plain and unadorned. But it is there for a reason. It signifies one of the most fundamental truths of the Christian faith: that we are welcome; that in the words of Jesus on the night before he died, "there is a place prepared for us" (see John 14:2). In Jesus, God has done everything that is needed for us to enjoy eternal life with him. That being welcomed into the life of God is symbolized by the table. As we shall see in a later session, it is also a foreshadowing of the banquet of heaven itself.

And Christian worship is very often gathered around the table in the service we call the Eucharist, Holy Communion, or The Lord's Supper. Like the very first Christians we worship by coming together to break bread (Acts 20.7). It is the basic act of Christian worship, instituted by Jesus himself on the night before he died. It is also very human. Meeting to eat is a wonderful way to bring people together. But it's not just the food itself that creates hospitality! Good hosts offer friendship too; the eating and being together around the table create that hospitable place, where conversations can occur and relationships develop.

Good hosts offer friendship too.

In the Eucharist God offers us such hospitality: God is the host, and we are the guests.

The service of Holy Communion has two distinct parts—

- **The Liturgy of the Word** (the readings from Scripture, the sermon, the Creed and the Intercessions).

- **The Liturgy of the Sacrament** (the Peace, the Preparation of the Table, the Great Prayer of Thanksgiving over the bread and wine, the Lord's Prayer, the breaking of the bread and the giving of Communion itself).

There are, as it were, two tables: the table where we gather to break open God's word; and the table where we gather to break open the bread. Around both these tables God gathers and feeds people.

In The Episcopal Church, the Eucharist often begins with the words, "Blessed be God: Father, Son, and Holy Spirit." God is taking the initiative. We gather around God's table and in God's presence. We don't need to invite God to join us. God is already here waiting to welcome us.

And, of course, God is everywhere—not just in church! God welcomes me wherever I am, so it is possible to worship anywhere and at any time. But the Eucharistic gathering of the Christian community is the place where this is made real. We Christians keep coming back to the table of the Lord because here we experience God's hospitality and here we learn to be hospitable ourselves.

> **In short**
> In the Eucharist, God is the host and we are the guests. We gather around God's table and learn from God's hospitality how to be hospitable ourselves.

For discussion

How has your life been enriched by hospitality? Share some experiences of welcoming others or being welcomed in yourself.

What elements in the worship you have attended remind you of God's welcome?

I am with you always

Sometimes it is easy to sense God's presence in worship. There is a description of a time like this in Exodus 15. The Israelites had just escaped from the oppressive regime in Egypt, and had experienced high drama as Moses led them through the Red Sea. They "saw the great work that the Lord did" and rejoiced at the signs of God's protection. Their enthusiastic song of praise and thanks was accompanied by tambourines and dancing. It was the very first "happy clappy" service!

But life isn't always like that! When the Israelites arrived in the desert, they didn't feel like worshiping God there. They struggled with the ongoing realities of daily life in a new situation, and it is not surprising that they reacted as they did. Grumbles and complaints like theirs are classic symptoms of what is sometimes called "culture shock"—the stresses that understandably occur when people have to adapt to new surroundings, bereft of a known way of life while simultaneously working out how to manage unfamiliar situations.

But God was already there in the desert—and welcomed them generously, just as they were. Manna was a completely unexpected gift, totally unplanned by them. All of them received God's generosity—not just a select few. As a whole community the Israelites were delivered from Egypt and fed in the desert, and this story became part of their "salvation history." In Psalm 78 we read how they retold this story together in worship to pass the memory down the generations. In John 6 Jesus too remembered this story and used it to talk about the gift that he brings to us.

Manna was a completely unexpected gift.

Whether the service is a Eucharist or not, meeting in worship can be a time when we are reminded of God's continuing welcome to us and of all that God has done to make that welcome possible. When we worship we retell the story of our faith. We remind ourselves of all the ways God has met with us. We bring to God our hopes and needs, our joys and fears. God is our gracious host. God doesn't just welcome everyone. God welcomes everything about us.

For discussion

How do you feel that God is with you when you worship?

What are the other times in your life when you have been aware of God's provision and welcome? How have these times become part of your own story? How is it changing you?

Journeying On

During this next week, think about how the welcome you receive from God in worship can be imitated in your daily life in the welcome and hospitality you offer to others—strangers as well as fellow pilgrims. We will share with each other any conclusions we have come to at the start of the next session. And if you haven't done so already, get a copy of the 1979 Book of Common Prayer from your local church and read through the service of Holy Eucharist. Rite I (pp. 323-340) offers traditional language and Rite II (pp. 355-366) has more contemporary language. Observe its structure and enjoy the beautiful language of its prayers.

Concluding Prayers

The cup of blessing that we bless,
is it not a sharing in the blood of Christ?
The bread that we break,
is it not a sharing in the body of Christ?
Because there is one bread,
we who are many are one body,
for we all partake of the one bread.

1 CORINTHIANS 10:16–17

Merciful God,
You have called us to your table.
Generous God,
You have fed us with the bread of life.
Abundant God,
Draw us and all people to the service of your Son;
And send us out to bring your peace and goodness to the world.
Amen.

Wisdom for the Journey

On Sundays we hold an assembly of all our members, whether they live in the city or in the outlying districts. The memoirs of the apostles or the writings of the prophets are read, as long as time permits. When the reader has finished, the president of the assembly speaks to us urging everyone to imitate the examples of virtue we have heard in the readings. Then we all stand up together and pray. When we have finished praying, bread and wine and water are brought forward. The president offers prayers and gives thanks as well as possible, and the people give their assent by saying: "Amen." Then follows the distribution of the food over which the prayer of thanksgiving has been recited; everyone present receives some, and the deacons take some to those who are absent. The wealthy, if they wish, may make a contribution— they, themselves, decide the amount. The collection is placed in the custody of the president, who uses it to help the orphans and widows and all who for any reason are in distress, whether because they are sick, in prison, or away from home.

JUSTIN (C. 100–165)

Do you wish to honor the body of the Savior? Then do not despise it when it is naked. Do not honor it in church with silk vestments while outside you are leaving it numb with cold and naked. He who said, "This is my body," and made it so by his word, is the same that said, "You saw me hungry and gave me no food. As you did it not to one of the least of my brothers and sisters, you did it not to me." Honor him by sharing your property with the poor. What God needs is not golden cups but golden hearts.

JOHN CHRYSOSTOM (C. 347–407)

The reason for our loving God *is* God. He is the initiator of our love and its final goal. God is loveable in himself and gives himself to us as the object of our love. He desires that our love for him should bring us happiness, and not be arid and barren. His love for us opens up inside us the way to love, and is the reward of our own reaching out in love. How gently he leads us in love's way, how generously he returns the love we give, how sweet he is to those who wait for him!

BERNARD OF CLAIRVAUX (1090–1153)

I hunger and I thirst:
Jesu, my manna be;
Ye living waters, burst
Out of the rock for me.

Thou bruised and broken Bread,
My life-long wants supply;
As living souls are fed,
O feed me, or I die.

J. S. B. MONSELL (1811–75)

The fundamental business of life is worship. At the root of all your being, your intellectual studies, the games you play, whatever it is, the impulse to do them well is and ought to be understood as being an impulse towards God, the source of all that is excellent. All life ought to be worship; and we know quite well there is no chance it will be worship unless we have times when we have worship and nothing else.

WILLIAM TEMPLE (1881–1944)

SESSION TWO:
THIS IS MY BODY BROKEN FOR YOU

In this session we look at the Eucharist as the pattern of all Christian worship.

Opening Prayers

I am the bread of life,
anyone who comes to me shall not hunger,
anyone who believes in me shall never thirst.
Alleluia. Lord, give us this bread always.

The bread of God comes down from heaven,
and gives life to the world.
Alleluia. Lord, give us this bread always.

Anyone who eats my flesh and drinks my blood has eternal life,
And I will raise him up on the last day.
Alleluia. Lord, give us this bread always.

It is the spirit that gives life; the flesh is of no avail.
the words I speak, they are spirit and they are life.
Alleluia. Lord, give us this bread always.

Walk with us, Lord,
Along the road of resurrection!
Explain for us, so slow to believe,
the things that scripture says of you.
Break the bread of the Eucharist with us
whenever we share our lives with our brothers and sisters.
Stay with us each time night approaches
and the daylight fades in our hearts.
Amen.

Conversation

Have you thought of any ways you can imitate God's hospitality in your daily life? Who are the strangers and fellow pilgrims that God might be asking you to show welcome to?

As a way into this session, share with each other any memories you have of significant meals in your life. Why were they important? What made them special?

Reflecting on Scripture

Reading

For I received from the Lord what I also handed on to you, that the Lord Jesus on the night when he was betrayed took a loaf of bread, ²⁴and when he had given thanks, he broke it and said, "This is my body that is for you. Do this in remembrance of me." ²⁵In the same way he took the cup also, after supper, saying, "This cup is the new covenant in my blood. Do this, as often as you drink it, in remembrance of me." ²⁶For as often as you eat this bread and drink the cup, you proclaim the Lord's death until he comes. ²⁷Whoever, therefore, eats the bread or drinks the cup of the Lord in an unworthy manner will be answerable for the body and blood of the Lord. ²⁸Examine yourselves, and only then eat of the bread and drink of the cup.

1 CORINTHIANS 11:23-28

Explanatory note

These words are often known as "the words of institution" because they command Jesus' followers to keep on remembering Jesus by breaking bread and sharing wine. They occur in slightly different forms here in 1 Corinthians 11:23-28 and in three out of the four Gospels (Matthew 26:26-29; Mark 14:22-25; Luke 22:19-21).

The words in 1 Corinthians are believed to have been the first ones written down (in approximately the mid-50s BCE, about 20 years or so before the words in the gospels reached their final form).

● Read the passage through once.

● Keep a few moments' silence.

● Read the passage a second time with different voices.

● Invite everyone to say aloud a word or phrase that strikes them.

● Read the passage a third time.

● Share together what this word or phrase might mean and what questions it raises.

Remembering

In a society that values bodily perfection, the invitation to break bread to remember a broken man is deeply countercultural. But this is precisely what Christians do every time they celebrate the Eucharist together. At the Last Supper, the bread that Jesus takes is broken so that it can be shared among the disciples. This simple, everyday act of breaking bread is not just a practical necessity to enable a group of first-century Jews to share food among themselves. Much more significantly, it points forward to the death by which Christ brings salvation to the world, and provides the means by which his followers will remember that death for generations to come. "Do this in remembrance of me" (1 Corinthians 11:24).

The celebration of Holy Communion is an act of the Church. We declare and remember the saving acts of God. It is something we do together—we are the priestly people of God. It is something that requires the presidency of an ordained minister—because the ordained minister, acting, as it were, as the representative of Christ, brings the universal to the local. The priest ensures that the service we offer is not just our private celebration but the one sacrifice of praise of the one, holy, catholic, and apostolic Church of Jesus Christ.

As we sift through our memories of past events and people we have known, it is easy to be forgetful or to become confused about some of the details. But then, prompted by something or someone, we can be reminded of them again. The Eucharist is different. We were not present at the Last Supper, nor did we stand with Mary and John at the foot of the cross. We're therefore not remembering something that we witnessed for ourselves first hand. Despite this obvious fact, Christians believe that, at the Eucharist, we remember Jesus and, as we do so, experience his presence among us. This remembering is much more profound than being reminded of a happy or sad event from our past, like a favorite holiday or the end of a relationship. At the

Eucharist, the memorial of Christ's death and resurrection is made possible through the transforming power of the Holy Spirit. The Spirit doesn't just remind us that Christ died and was raised on the third day, but enables us to be transformed again and again by the events of Good Friday and Easter. In this way we become more fully the people God calls us to be. Those who, through baptism, have died to sin and been raised to new life with Christ (see Romans 6:5-11) experience this transformation again and again as the Eucharist is celebrated together as members of the Church, which Paul describes as the body of Christ (see 1 Corinthians 12:27).

In short

When we remember Jesus in the Eucharist, we are transformed again and again by Jesus' death and resurrection and so become more fully the people that God wants us to be.

For discussion

As you have begun to grow in the Christian life, what does the Eucharist and receiving Holy Communion mean to you?

What are you remembering?

How important is it for you to remember the death and resurrection of Jesus when you worship at the Eucharist or at any other service for that matter?

A sacrifice of praise

Like the apostles who were invited by Jesus to share a meal with him on the night before his death, whenever we respond to Jesus' invitation to "do this in remembrance of me," he promises to be with us and to feed us with his body and blood. He does this to bring us into communion with him and with our fellow Christians, strengthening us with his presence as we seek to live as his disciples. "For as often as you eat this bread and drink the cup, you proclaim the Lord's death until he comes" (1 Corinthians 11:26).

Jesus' death is a sacrifice motivated by love.

For Christians, Jesus' death on the cross is a sacrifice—a sacrifice motivated by love. As Jesus says in John's Gospel, "No one has greater love than this, to lay down one's life for one's friends" (John 15:13).

But how do we know it is a sacrifice? Well, Jesus' actions—taking and breaking the bread and pouring out the wine—are like an acted parable. Although the disciples would not have understood it at the time, Jesus is giving them a way of interpreting his death correctly. Like the bread broken, Jesus' body is broken on the cross. Like the wine poured out, Jesus' blood is shed for us.

There can be no repetition of Jesus' sacrifice, but whenever we celebrate the Eucharist we are in communion with the risen Christ whose sacrifice has brought us peace with God. This is why the table around which we gather is also called an altar, a place where the sacrifice of Christ is recalled and its benefits made present.

To participate in the Eucharist is to recognize our brokenness (individual and communal), and our need to unite with Christ to be made whole. As we explored in other sessions in *Pilgrim*, Christians believe that Jesus was broken to save us from our sins and brokenness. We now offer the bread and cup to God as a sacrifice of praise and thanksgiving. Made whole through communion with Christ's sacrificial death, we offer our lives to God as a living sacrifice. The words offered during the prayer blessing the bread and wine in Rite I (BCP p. 336) expresses it this way: "And here we offer and present unto thee, O Lord, our selves, our souls and bodies, to be a reasonable, holy, and living sacrifice unto thee."

This is true of all worship; even the simplest song of a few Christians gathered in a classroom or the grandest service you can possibly imagine is an offering of praise, the sacrifice of our hearts and the alignment of our lives to God. As we gather around Christ's table, the one whom we remember offers us a piece of his broken body to make us whole, and sends us out as members of his body to share his life in the brokenness of the world.

> **In short**
>
> When we participate in the Eucharist, we recall Jesus' sacrifice for us, recognize our own brokenness, remember that he was broken to make us whole, and offer him our souls and bodies as a sacrifice of thanksgiving for all he has done for us.

For discussion

- What does sacrificial living mean to you and your Christian community?

- How does worship, and especially the Eucharist, help you live the Christian life and offer your life as a sacrifice of praise?

- How does the double symbolism of table and altar help you think about the different ways we experience the Eucharist?

Journeying On

During this next week, think about how we are called to live out the sacrificial love we see in the death and resurrection of Jesus and which is made present for us in the Eucharist. What does it mean for us to live sacrificial lives? What sacrifices might God be asking you to make?

Concluding Prayers

**The cup of blessing that we bless,
is it not a sharing in the blood of Christ?
The bread that we break,
is it not a sharing in the body of Christ?
Because there is one bread,
we who are many are one body,
for we all partake of the one bread.**

1 CORINTHIANS 10:16-17

Merciful God,
You have called us to your table.
Generous God,
You have fed us with the bread of life.
Abundant God,
Draw us and all people to the service of your Son;
And send us out to bring your peace and goodness to the world.
Amen.

Wisdom for the Journey

We do not consume the eucharistic bread and wine as if it were ordinary food and drink. We have been taught that just as Jesus Christ became a human being of flesh and blood by the power of the Word of God for our salvation, so also the food that our flesh and blood assimilate for their nourishment becomes the flesh and blood of this Jesus who became flesh by the power of his word in the prayer of thanksgiving.

JUSTIN (C. 100–165)

I came to see that there is no space without God: space does not exist apart from God. God is in heaven, in hell, and beyond the seas. God lives in everything and enfolds everything. God embraces all that is, and is embraced by the universe: confined to no part within it, he encompasses all that exists. My soul drew joy from contemplating the mystery of God's wisdom, his sheer majesty, and I worshiped the eternity and immeasurable greatness of my Father and creator.

HILARY OF POITIERS (315–67)

Believers know the body of Christ if they do not neglect to be the body of Christ.

AUGUSTINE (354–430)

Love is that liquor sweet and most divine,
Which my God feels as blood; but I, as wine.

GEORGE HERBERT (1593–1633)

HE WAS MADE KNOWN TO THEM IN THE BREAKING OF THE BREAD

pilgrim

In this session we look at the intimacy we have with God in Holy Communion and how we are transformed by the encounter.

Opening Prayers

I am the bread of life,
anyone who comes to me shall not hunger,
anyone who believes in me shall never thirst.
Alleluia. Lord, give us this bread always.

The bread of God comes down from heaven,
and gives life to the world.
Alleluia. Lord, give us this bread always.

Anyone who eats my flesh and drinks my blood has eternal life,
And I will raise him up on the last day.
Alleluia. Lord, give us this bread always.

It is the spirit that gives life; the flesh is of no avail.
the words I speak, they are spirit and they are life.
Alleluia. Lord, give us this bread always.

Walk with us, Lord,
Along the road of resurrection!
Explain for us, so slow to believe,
the things that scripture says of you.
Break the bread of the Eucharist with us
whenever we share our lives with our brothers and sisters.
Stay with us each time night approaches
and the daylight fades in our hearts.
Amen.

Conversation

Share with each other your thoughts about how God might be asking us to live sacrificially. Then, in preparation for this session, share any experiences of an encounter that transformed you. It will probably be with another person. What happened? What was it about this person that was so transformative?

Reflecting on Scripture

Reading

Now on that same day two of them were going to a village called Emmaus, about seven miles from Jerusalem, ¹⁴and talking with each other about all these things that had happened. ¹⁵While they were talking and discussing, Jesus himself came near and went with them, ¹⁶but their eyes were kept from recognizing him. ¹⁷And he said to them, "What are you discussing with each other while you walk along?" They stood still, looking sad. ¹⁸Then one of them, whose name was Cleopas, answered him, "Are you the only stranger in Jerusalem who does not know the things that have taken place there in these days?" ¹⁹He asked them, "What things?" They replied, "The things about Jesus of Nazareth, who was a prophet mighty in deed and word before God and all the people, ²⁰and how our chief priests and leaders handed him over to be condemned to death and crucified him. ²¹But we had hoped that he was the one to redeem Israel. Yes, and besides all this, it is now the third day since these things took place. ²²Moreover, some women of our group astounded us. They were at the tomb early this morning, ²³and when they did not find his body there, they came back and told us that they had indeed seen a vision of angels who said that he was alive. ²⁴Some of those who were with us went to the tomb and found it just as the women had said; but they did not see him." ²⁵Then he said to them, "Oh, how foolish you are, and how slow of heart to believe all that the prophets have declared! ²⁶Was it not necessary that the Messiah should suffer these things and then enter into his glory?" ²⁷Then beginning with Moses and all the prophets, he interpreted to them the things about himself in all the scriptures.
²⁸As they came near the village to which they were going, he walked ahead as if he were going on. ²⁹But they urged him strongly, saying, "Stay with us, because it is almost evening and the day is now nearly over." So he went in to stay with them. ³⁰When he was at the table with them, he took bread, blessed

and broke it, and gave it to them. ³¹Then their eyes were opened, and they recognized him; and he vanished from their sight. ³²They said to each other, "Were not our hearts burning within us while he was talking to us on the road, while he was opening the scriptures to us?" ³³That same hour they got up and returned to Jerusalem; and they found the eleven and their companions gathered together. ³⁴They were saying, "The Lord has risen indeed, and he has appeared to Simon!" ³⁵Then they told what had happened on the road, and how he had been made known to them in the breaking of the bread.

LUKE 24:13-35

- Read the passage through once—though as this is a longer passage than usual you may decide to omit the first reading.

- Keep a few moments' silence.

- Read the passage a second time with different voices.

- Invite everyone to say aloud a word or phrase that strikes them.

- Read the passage a third time.

- Share together what this word or phrase might mean and what questions it raises.

Reflection   ANGELA TILBY

The Eucharist transforms our lives

All Christian worship is, potentially, an encounter with the risen Lord. In worship, God calls us into a future that is already God's, and we offer ourselves to be transformed. The Eucharist, perhaps more than any other form of Christian worship, makes this transformation vivid and real because it brings us directly into Christ's presence, not only through Scripture, but by a kind of remembering that makes his Easter victory present to us. The bread and wine—ordinary food and drink— become charged with the memory of Christ's death and resurrection. For some this is focused in the bread and wine itself. The consecrated bread and wine are lifted up so that people can see that "the Lord is here." For others the bread and wine act as reminders that point to the Lord's spiritual presence with us. This presence of Jesus in Holy Communion is called a sacrament, which, as we shall see in a later session, is an "outward and visible sign of an inward and spiritual grace." How this happens has been disputed by Christians over the centuries and has, sadly, led to some divisions between different branches of the Church.

This explains the various ways the Eucharist is celebrated, the varying importance that different Christians give to it, and even the fact that we have more than one name for the service. But all Christians of whatever tradition unite around this truth: the Lord who died on the cross for us opens his arms and longs to feeds us with his risen life. Jesus is the one "in whom all our hungers are satisfied." We celebrate this story of transforming love with Holy Communion and in our worship.

In The Episcopal Church, all who are baptized, no matter the denomination, are welcome to receive Holy Communion, including children. As Leonel Mitchell has framed it, "It is through baptism that the mighty saving acts of Christ become available to us. It is birth into that new life in Christ… Then the Eucharist is the sacramental proclamation and celebration of that covenant relationship… Baptism…is the basis of the relationship which the Eucharist celebrates." Since we meet and receive Jesus in Holy Communion, we need to prepare ourselves. This involves examining our lives, repenting of our sins, and being in love and charity with all people. We should also pray before we come to church, asking God to make our hearts ready to receive the bread and wine, body and blood. In the course of our Christian development, we grow in our understanding and commitment to the responsibilities of our Baptism. If we choose, we can be Confirmed and receive the laying-on-of-hands by a bishop as a symbol of our reaffirmation. No matter our age, all are welcome to receive Holy Communion.

The story of the Emmaus road underscores this theme. The disciples of Jesus are living with unmet hopes and deep grief. They meet a stranger on the road who walks alongside them. In his company they find they are able to tell their story and to express their sorrows and regret. Jesus listens to all that they have to say and then responds to them, opening the Scriptures and helping them to see that his death has not been the end of everything, but the moment of true liberation and transformation. Then, at the meal that they share together, he breaks bread—and they see him as he really is. The risen Christ meets them in the breaking of the bread. They cannot sustain the vision—Christ vanishes from their sight. But they are changed: "Were not our hearts burning within us while he was talking to us on the road, while he was opening the scriptures to us?" Their hunger for hope, meaning, and restoration is satisfied.

> **In short**
>
> Christians have many different views of the Eucharist, but we are all united in believing that the Jesus who died on the cross for us is the one in whom all our hungers are satisfied.

For discussion

When you worship, how are you aware of Christ's risen presence?

And what sort of worship makes your heart burn within you?

Eucharistic living

As with all Christian worship—be it the simplest service of the Word, a pentecostal extravaganza, or Holy Communion itself—we come as the selves that we are, with our particular strengths and weaknesses, virtues, and frailties. We bring with us the whole network of relationships in which we live and work and struggle and dream. All this is raw material for transformation and is symbolized by the bread and wine, the work of human hands.

We come as the selves that we are.

But we are not present merely as individuals. Like the disciples on the Emmaus road, we come in company with one another, with shared memories, doubts, and hopes. Together we praise God and confess our need of God's goodness and grace in our lives. The risen Christ draws near to us as he did on the Emmaus road, and we hear his promise to us in the Gospel. Then we see and hear how Jesus took the bread, blessed it, broke it and gave it to his disciples. The ordinary fabric of our lives is taken up into Christ's risen life and given back to us, charged with the hope and joy that comes from God's future. The Eucharist transforms us into kingdom people who are called to share our bread with the hungry and bring life and hope to the world.

In the Eucharist we are always being made new. This is beautifully expressed in the special prayer, the "Collect" for the Second Sunday after the feast of the Epiphany:

> Almighty God, whose Son our Savior Jesus Christ is the light of the world: Grant that your people, illumined by your Word and Sacraments, may shine with the radiance of Christ's glory, that he may be known, worshiped, and obeyed to the ends of the earth; through Jesus Christ our Lord, who with you and the Holy Spirit lives and reigns, one God, now and for ever. Amen.

In short

In the Eucharist, we do not come just as individuals but with all our networks of relationships. There the whole of our lives are caught up into the life of the risen Christ and given back to us renewed.

For discussion

How do you think you should prepare for worship? And how would you advise others?

Jesus took bread, blessed it, broke it, and gave it. How might this be a pattern for Christian living?

Journeying On

During this next week, think how worship forms your life and shapes who you are. How might God be taking, blessing, breaking, and using you in God's service? Ponder each word carefully. Take. Bless. Break. Share. How is this happening in your life? How is God transforming you? How does God want to increase it within you so that your life mirrors the offering of Christ?

Concluding Prayers

The cup of blessing that we bless,
is it not a sharing in the blood of Christ?
The bread that we break,
is it not a sharing in the body of Christ?
Because there is one bread,
we who are many are one body,
for we all partake of the one bread.

1 CORINTHIANS 10:16-17

Merciful God,
You have called us to your table.
Generous God,
You have fed us with the bread of life.
Abundant God,
Draw us and all people to the service of your Son;
And send us out to bring your peace and goodness to the world.
Amen.

Wisdom for the Journey

In the same way that earthly bread, having received the invocation of God, is no longer ordinary bread but Eucharist, made up of two components, one earthly and the other heavenly, so our bodies that share in the Eucharist are no longer corruptible because they have the hope of resurrection.

IRENAEUS (130–C. 200)

Calling her children around her the Church nourishes them with holy milk, that is with the infant Word… The Word is everything to a child; both Father and Mother, both instructor and nurse. "Eat my flesh," he says, and "Drink my blood." The Lord supplies us with these intimate nutrients. He delivers over his flesh and pours out his blood and nothing is lacking for the growth of his children. O incredible mystery!

CLEMENT OF ALEXANDRIA (150–215)

When you approach the altar, do not present your hands spread out or your fingers separated, but instead make a throne with your left hand for your right hand since it is to receive the King, and receiving the body of Christ in the hollow of your hand, say "Amen."

CYRIL OF JERUSALEM (C. 315–386)

At Emmaus the two disciples set the table, serve the food, and in the breaking of bread discover the God whom they failed to come to know in the explanation of the scriptures. It was not in hearing the precepts of God that they were enlightened, but when they carried them out.

GREGORY THE GREAT (540–604)

Soul of Christ, sanctify me,
body of Christ, save me,
blood of Christ, inebriate me,
water from the side of Christ, wash me.
Passion of Jesus, strengthen me.
O good Jesus, hear me:
hide me within your wounds
and let me never be separated from you.
From the wicked enemy defend me,
in the hour of my death, call me
and bid me come to you,
so that with your saints I may praise you
for ever and ever. Amen.

ANONYMOUS (FOURTEENTH CENTURY)

The country parson being to administer the sacraments, is at a
stand with himself, how or what behavior to assume for so holy
things. Especially at communion times he is in a great confusion,
as being not only to receive God, but to break and administer him.
Neither finds he any issue in this, but to throw himself down at the
throne of grace, saying "Lord, thou knowest what thou didst when
thou appointedst it to be done thus; therefore do thou fulfill what
thou didst appoint; for thou art not only the feast, but the way to it."

GEORGE HERBERT (1593–1633)

Here our humblest homage pay we;
Here in loving reverence bow;
Here for faith's discernment pray we,
Lest we fail to know thee now.
Alleluya,
Thou art here, we ask not how.

G. H. BOURNE (1840–1925)

SESSION FOUR:
IF YOU HEAR MY VOICE AND OPEN THE DOOR,
I WILL COME IN AND EAT WITH YOU

pilgrim

In this session we look at worship as a sign and foretaste
of heaven.

Opening Prayers

I am the bread of life,
anyone who comes to me shall not hunger,
anyone who believes in me shall never thirst.
Alleluia. Lord, give us this bread always.

The bread of God comes down from heaven,
and gives life to the world.
Alleluia. Lord, give us this bread always.

Anyone who eats my flesh and drinks my blood has eternal life,
And I will raise him up on the last day.
Alleluia. Lord, give us this bread always.

It is the spirit that gives life; the flesh is of no avail.
the words I speak, they are spirit and they are life.
Alleluia. Lord, give us this bread always.

Walk with us, Lord,
Along the road of resurrection!
Explain for us, so slow to believe,
the things that scripture says of you.
Break the bread of the Eucharist with us
whenever we share our lives with our brothers and sisters.
Stay with us each time night approaches
and the daylight fades in our hearts.
Amen.

Conversation

How do you think worship shapes your life? Have you been able to think of ways God is blessing, breaking, and using you?

Then for this session turn your minds to thoughts of heaven. When you think of heaven, what images come to mind? Share them with each other.

Reflecting on Scripture

Reading

"I know your works; you are neither cold nor hot. I wish that you were either cold or hot. [16]So, because you are lukewarm, and neither cold nor hot, I am about to spit you out of my mouth. [17]For you say, 'I am rich, I have prospered, and I need nothing.' You do not realize that you are wretched, pitiable, poor, blind, and naked. [18]Therefore I counsel you to buy from me gold refined by fire so that you may be rich; and white robes to clothe you and to keep the shame of your nakedness from being seen; and salve to anoint your eyes so that you may see. [19]I reprove and discipline those whom I love. Be earnest, therefore, and repent. [20]Listen! I am standing at the door, knocking; if you hear my voice and open the door, I will come in to you and eat with you, and you with me. [21]To the one who conquers I will give a place with me on my throne, just as I myself conquered and sat down with my Father on his throne. [22]Let anyone who has an ear listen to what the Spirit is saying to the churches."

REVELATION 3:15-22

Explanatory note

The start of the book of Revelation takes the form of letters to seven different churches in Asia Minor (what we would now call Turkey). One of these letters was to the church in Laodicea, well known for its water supply, which was lukewarm.

● Read the passage through once.

● Keep a few moments' silence.

● Read the passage a second time with different voices.

● Invite everyone to say aloud a word or phrase that strikes them.

● Read the passage a third time.

● Share together what this word or phrase might mean and what questions it raises.

Reflection

JOHN INGE

A sign and foretaste of the banquet of heaven

What will heaven be like? Christians have generally seemed to spend more time arguing about who will be admitted to heaven than thinking about its character. What, though, do we know about the nature of heaven? A moment's reflection reminds us that we have been told by Jesus himself that heaven is the place where God reigns, the place of God's kingdom. When we pray as he taught, we ask that "God's kingdom will come on earth as it is in heaven." And what is God's kingdom like? The Scriptures give us all sorts of images of the kingdom, many of which involve a feast. One of the recurring pictures of heaven and of humanity redeemed is that of a feast. "On this mountain the Lord of hosts will make a feast of rich food, a feast of well-aged wines," proclaims the prophet Isaiah (Isaiah 25:6). As Jesus puts it, "I tell you, many will come from east and west and will eat with Abraham and Isaac and Jacob in the kingdom of heaven" (Matthew 8:11).

Feasting is how we celebrate great occasions.

That the kingdom of heaven should have been pictured as a feast in biblical times when food was often scarce is hardly surprising. Even today, though, when many of us in the affluent West have much more food than we need, the image of the feast is still a powerful one. Feasting is how we celebrate great occasions—as is evidenced by the way food dominates television ads before Christmas. In a feast, what is at least as important as the food and drink, though, is the people with whom we share it. Eating and drinking on your own is no feast. Jesus proclaims to his disciples that he will drink the cup *with them* in the kingdom. Perhaps the best image we have of heaven, then, is of eating and drinking at a feast with Jesus and all the redeemed in the kingdom.

Therefore, since the earliest times, Christians have believed that at the Eucharist we receive a foretaste of this kingdom feast. For it was at the Last Supper when Jesus was giving us the Eucharist that he talked to his disciples about drinking the cup with them in the kingdom (Matthew 26:29).

The Episcopal Church expects Christians to receive Holy Communion at least three times a year—Christmas, Easter, and one other time. Most churches celebrate Communion on Sunday as their principal service; a few offer Eucharist on other week days.

The usual method for receiving Holy Communion is to place one open hand upon another, so that the consecrated bread can be safely and easily placed in the center of the palm. With your hand, the chalice (cup of wine) should be guided to your lips to take a sip. Some Christians prefer to hold onto the bread (or wafer) and dip it into the chalice. This is called intinction. After receiving each element, it is common to say "Amen" following the words "the Body of Christ..." and "the Blood of Christ..."

However we receive Communion, Jesus is present. The Church has understood this in different ways through the centuries, sometimes generating painful disputes. At one end of the spectrum, Christians have believed that the bread and wine become the body and blood of Jesus. At the other, what we do is a memorial meal in which Jesus is present in the gathered community that remember him. Between these is the view sometimes referred to as the "real presence," declaring that the bread remains bread and the wine remains wine but take on new value and meaning that is the presence of Jesus.

We have spoken about the Eucharist in this way throughout Christian history. The Holy Communion we share in church is not the fullness of the feast itself but a taste—a glimpse and effective sign of wonders to come, glory to be revealed. We live between "already" and "not yet"; we eat and drink with the risen Christ and receive his presence "until he comes again" (1 Corinthians 11:26). We receive the bread of the world to come (John 6:48), the new wine of the kingdom (Luke 5:37).

> **In short**
> One of the descriptions in the Bible of the glorious future God promises for God's people is that of a great feast—in the Eucharist we get a glimpse of the feast that God promises to us all.

For discussion

- What do you think the heavenly feast will be like?
- How does our worship on earth prepare us?

The bread of tomorrow

Have you ever wondered why, in the Lord's Prayer, Jesus said "Give us today our daily bread" rather than "Give us today our bread" or "Give us our daily bread"? The two words translated as "day" and "daily" are different in the Greek and the sentence might better be rendered "Give us today our tomorrow's bread." What does that mean? It could be "the bread that has the character of the future feast." That's what Early Church Fathers such as Cyprian and Jerome suggested when they translated it as "Give us this day our supernatural or supersubstantial bread." In other words, we are asking that we should be given the bread that we shall receive at the Heavenly Feast. In the Lord's Prayer, then, we pray for the things that make up the kingdom: the hallowing of God's name, the coming of God's reign, the forgiveness of sins, and the food of heaven.

It is the totality of our humanity that is redeemed.

The Eucharist is a foretaste of the kingdom, a wonderful one that involves all of our humanity—body, mind, and spirit. This reminds us that it is the totality of our humanity that is redeemed. Christ comes to us not just in the head (rationally), not just through our heart (emotionally), but physically—"God in the gut"as Graham Greene put it. By this heavenly food we are given the strength not only to pray but to labor for the kingdom of God of which we receive a foretaste.

In short

In the Lord's Prayer we ask that God will give us our "daily bread." This might mean that we are asking God to give us tomorrow's bread today—in other words, to give us a taste of our heavenly food.

For discussion

- Have you ever felt that in worship the life of tomorrow is breaking in to today? What was it like? What difference does it make?

- What is it about the Eucharist that feels like a feast to you?

Journeying On

Start thinking about your own pattern of worship. Do you attend each week? Do you need to establish a rule about this? What about the major festivals of the Christian year? Would it be a good idea to decide that these are times when you also should be gathered with God's people around the Lord's Table?

Concluding Prayers

**The cup of blessing that we bless,
is it not a sharing in the blood of Christ?
The bread that we break,
is it not a sharing in the body of Christ?
Because there is one bread,
we who are many are one body,
for we all partake of the one bread.**

1 CORINTHIANS 10:16-17

Merciful God,
You have called us to your table.
Generous God,
You have fed us with the bread of life.
Abundant God,
**Draw us and all people to the service of your Son;
And send us out to bring your peace and goodness to the world.
Amen.**

Wisdom for the Journey

As this broken bread once scattered over the mountains has been gathered together to make a single loaf, so Lord gather your church together from the ends of the earth into your kingdom.

ANONYMOUS (LATE FIRST CENTURY)

Just as Scripture describes the unity of the faithful in the words: "They were of one mind and heart in God," so the image of the wine functions in the same way as that of the kneading of many grains into one visible loaf. Think how wine is made. Many grapes hang on the vine in clusters, but their juice flows together into an indivisible liquid once they are crushed. It was in these images that Christ our Lord signified to us that we should belong to him, when he hallowed the sacrament of our peace and unity on his table.

AUGUSTINE (354–430)

Christ gave us the Eucharist that we might by it attain unto endless day and the very table of Christ, and there [in heaven] receive in fullness and unto all satisfaction that of which we have been given the taste.

PETER CHRYSOLOGUS, FIFTH CENTURY

Let us receive Christ at our table now so as to be welcomed at his eternal banquet. Let us show hospitality to Christ present in the stranger now so that at the judgement he will not ignore us as strangers, but will welcome us as brothers and sisters into his kingdom.

GREGORY THE GREAT (540–604)

DO THIS TO REMEMBER ME

pilgrim

In this session we look at how worship shapes the whole of life.

Opening Prayers

I am the bread of life,
anyone who comes to me shall not hunger,
anyone who believes in me shall never thirst.
Alleluia. Lord, give us this bread always.

The bread of God comes down from heaven,
and gives life to the world.
Alleluia. Lord, give us this bread always.

Anyone who eats my flesh and drinks my blood has eternal life,
And I will raise him up on the last day.
Alleluia. Lord, give us this bread always.

It is the spirit that gives life; the flesh is of no avail.
The words I speak, they are spirit and they are life.
Alleluia. Lord, give us this bread always.

Walk with us, Lord,
Along the road of resurrection!
Explain for us, so slow to believe,
the things that scripture says of you.
Break the bread of the Eucharist with us
whenever we share our lives with our brothers and sisters.
Stay with us each time night approaches
and the daylight fades in our hearts.
Amen.

Conversation

What do you think is a reasonable and realistic pattern for daily prayer and worship? What should all Christians aspire to? What will your pattern be?

Then in preparation for this session think about the things we actually worship. If worship means literally, "the things we give worth to," what are the things that actually take first place in your life?

Reflecting on Scripture

Reading

He said to them, "I have eagerly desired to eat this Passover with you before I suffer; [16]for I tell you, I will not eat it until it is fulfilled in the kingdom of God." [17]Then he took a cup, and after giving thanks he said, "Take this and divide it among yourselves; [18]for I tell you that from now on I will not drink of the fruit of the vine until the kingdom of God comes." [19]Then he took a loaf of bread, and when he had given thanks, he broke it and gave it to them, saying, "This is my body, which is given for you. Do this in remembrance of me." [20]And he did the same with the cup after supper, saying, "This cup that is poured out for you is the new covenant in my blood."

LUKE 22:15-20

Explanatory note

This is the version of the words of institution from Luke's Gospel (compare them with the ones from 1 Corinthians 11 that we saw in Session 2).

Notice that Luke's words have Jesus sharing two cups: one before the breaking of the bread and one after it. These two cups may be connected to two out of the four cups associated with the Jewish Passover meal.

- Read the passage through once.
- Keep a few moments' silence.
- Read the passage a second time with different voices.
- Invite everyone to say aloud a word or phrase that strikes them.
- Read the passage a third time.
- Share together what this word or phrase might mean and what questions it raises.

Community with God

Against all the beguiling philosophies of the world, the Christian faith makes this great claim: I worship, therefore I am.

At the heart of the Christian faith is the belief that we are made for community in God. "The human heart is restless," wrote Augustine, "until it finds its rest in God." When we worship we become the people who find their rest and fulfillment in God. We become who we are meant to be. We enter into community with the God who, in Jesus, is revealed as a community of persons, Father, Son, and Holy Spirit. This is the community that we are part of through our baptism. The Church is the community of persons who have been gathered together by Christ and have access to God. And worship is what we do.

Of course, it doesn't always feel like this when we worship. Sometimes we are distracted. Sometimes it is boring. Sometimes we don't know the hymns or are put off by the sermon. But it is still true. When we worship we enter deeply into that relationship with God that Jesus has made possible by his death and resurrection.

In The Episcopal Church there are many, many different types and styles of worship. But they are all doing the same thing: offering a sacrifice of thanks and praise to God. There are services called Morning Prayer, Evening Prayer, and Compline where we gather around the table of the Word, search the Scriptures, confess our sins, and sing God's praises. These services do not need to be led by an ordained minister, and are often led by a lay person who has been trained and licensed as a Worship Leader or Preacher. Sometimes worship is completely sung, including the prayers. Some churches use incense and bells as an expression of prayer in worship. However, the presiding minister of the Eucharist will always be a priest, and it is the job of the clergy and Vestry (church council) of a congregation to have oversight of worship to ensure that what is celebrated and taught is the faith of Jesus Christ.

The Eucharist is the primary act of worship in the Church, the one service given us by Jesus himself. But as we have seen, it is also the pattern for all worship. Every time Christian people gather for worship, break open God's word, enjoy fellowship together, and confess their need of God, then we are entering into the life of heaven. We are joining our voices with those of the saints and the angels who forever sing God's praises. We participate in the life to come. The life of tomorrow breaks into the life of today.

> **In short**
> When we worship we enter deeply into that relationship with God that Jesus made possible by his death and resurrection and are joining our voices with the saints and the angels who worship God continually.

For discussion

What worship works best for you?

Continue to think about your own pattern for worship and daily prayer. Discuss this with others, and begin to make some conclusions for your own life as a disciple of Christ.

Becoming what you worship

Worship changes us. This is why the Bible is so forceful in its condemnation of idolatry. If you worship something that isn't God—money or power for instance—then there is a very real danger that you will become like the thing you worship. But if we worship God... If we sing God's praises... If we look long and lovingly at Jesus... If we receive his words of forgiveness, his bread of life, then we become like him. "All of us, with unveiled faces, seeing the glory of the Lord...are being transformed into the same image," says Paul (2 Corinthians 3:18).

It is for all these reasons that we must take worship very seriously. It's not that God needs our praises; rather we need to be made people who are thankful and adoring. (We are far too easily in love with ourselves!)

And because we are made for heaven, we are made for worship. It should be our joyful duty to be part of the worshipping community of our local church every Sunday. We should also try to observe the major festivals of the church year, especially Christmas (with the feast of the Incarnation) and Holy Week and Easter (when we recall Christ's passion, death, and resurrection). We should make sure that we receive Holy Communion as regularly as we can, and always at Christmas and Easter. As we have explored, the sacraments are channels of grace and living encounters with the risen Christ.

Finally, Scripture also has some stern warnings about worship. "I despise your festivals," says God, "Take away from me the noise of your songs; I will not listen to the melody of your harps. But let justice roll down like waters, and righteousness like an ever-flowing stream" (Amos 5:21, 23-24). For unless worship is changing us so that our concerns and priorities are shaped by the concerns and priorities of God, and unless we are seeking God's justice and righteousness for the world, then our worship is worthless.

> **In short**
> We worship God not because God needs it or because it changes God, but because it changes us.

For discussion

- How might God be scandalized or despairing of the Church and its worship today?

- How does worship at our church shape our priorities and concerns in the world?

Journeying On

During this next week, think about how worship is changing the priorities and concerns of your life and what your response should be. How would you tell someone this story of what God has done in Christ and how this is experienced and lived out in worship? Be ready to share this with others in the group next time.

Concluding Prayers

The cup of blessing that we bless,
is it not a sharing in the blood of Christ?
The bread that we break,
is it not a sharing in the body of Christ?
Because there is one bread,
we who are many are one body,
for we all partake of the one bread.

1 CORINTHIANS 10:16-17

Merciful God,
You have called us to your table.
Generous God,
You have fed us with the bread of life.
Abundant God,
Draw us and all people to the service of your Son;
And send us out to bring your peace and goodness to the world.
Amen.

Wisdom for the Journey

Hasten to the springs, draw from the wells. In God alone is the wellspring of life, a spring whose waters will never fail you. In his light is to be found a light that nothing can darken. So desire that light which your eyes know not! Your inward eye is preparing to see the light. Your inward thirst burns to be quenched at the spring.

AUGUSTINE (354–430)

It is possible to regard worship as one of the greatest of humanity's mistakes; a form taken by the fantasy-life, the desperate effort of bewildered creatures to come to terms with the surrounding mystery. Or it may be accepted as the most profound of man's responses to reality; and more than this, the organ of his divine knowledge and the earnest of eternal life.

EVELYN UNDERHILL (1875–1941)

Was ever another command so obeyed? For century after century, spreading slowly to every continent and country and among every race on earth, this action has been done, in every conceivable human circumstance, for every conceivable human need from infancy and before it to extreme old age and after it, from the pinnacles of earthly greatness to the refuge of fugitives in the caves and dens of the earth. Men have found no better thing than this to do for kings at their crowning and for criminals going to the scaffold; for armies in triumph or for a bride and bridegroom in a little country church; for the proclamation of a dogma or for a good crop of wheat; for the wisdom of the parliament of a mighty nation or for a sick old woman afraid to die; for a schoolboy sitting an examination or for Columbus setting out to discover America; for the famine of whole provinces or for the soul of a dead lover. One could fill many pages with the reasons why men have done this, and not tell a hundredth part of them. And best of all, week by week and month by month, on a hundred thousand successive Sundays, faithfully, unfailingly, across all the parishes of Christendom, the pastors have done this just to *make* the *plebs sancta Dei*—the holy common people of God.

GREGORY DIX (1901–52)

The Risen Jesus who is the heart of the heavenly worship is also the Jesus who was crucified, and we share in heaven's worship only as sharing also in the Jesus who suffers in the world around us, reminding us to meet him there and to serve him in those who suffer.

MICHAEL RAMSEY (1904–88)

SESSION SIX:
I AM THE BREAD OF LIFE

pilgrim

In this session we look at the notion that the whole of life is sacramental.

Opening Prayers

I am the bread of life,
anyone who comes to me shall not hunger,
anyone who believes in me shall never thirst.
Alleluia. Lord, give us this bread always.

The bread of God comes down from heaven,
and gives life to the world.
Alleluia. Lord, give us this bread always.

Anyone who eats my flesh and drinks my blood has eternal life,
And I will raise him up on the last day.
Alleluia. Lord, give us this bread always.

It is the spirit that gives life; the flesh is of no avail.
the words I speak, they are spirit and they are life.
Alleluia. Lord, give us this bread always.

Walk with us, Lord,
Along the road of resurrection!
Explain for us, so slow to believe,
the things that scripture says of you.
Break the bread of the Eucharist with us
whenever we share our lives with our brothers and sisters.
Stay with us each time night approaches
and the daylight fades in our hearts.
Amen.

Conversation

Share with each other as a way of summing up all that we have explored in this course the things that God has done for you in Christ that you particularly experience in worship. You might also like to mention where you have seen and encountered God in daily life, and what you think your future pattern of worship and daily prayer will be. Allow this session more time than usual and give each person in the group a chance to speak.

Reflecting on Scripture

Reading

Jesus said to them, "I am the bread of life. Whoever comes to me will never be hungry, and whoever believes in me will never be thirsty. [36]But I said to you that you have seen me and yet do not believe. [37]Everything that the Father gives me will come to me, and anyone who comes to me I will never drive away; [38]for I have come down from heaven, not to do my own will, but the will of him who sent me. [39]And this is the will of him who sent me, that I should lose nothing of all that he has given me, but raise it up on the last day."

JOHN 6:35-39

● Read the passage through once.

● Keep a few moments' silence.

● Read the passage a second time with different voices.

● Invite everyone to say aloud a word or phrase that strikes them.

● Read the passage a third time.

● Share together what this word or phrase might mean and what questions it raises.

Reflection   JOHN PRITCHARD

The sacramental principle

God uses material things as signs and pledges of grace, and as a means by which we receive them. More than anywhere else we see this principle lived out in the life of Jesus himself. Jesus is the outward and visible sign of God's presence in the world always and everywhere. He was the human face of God, God's self-portrait. Quite simply, like Father, like Son.

Jesus seems to be claiming such a special sacramental identity when he says in John's Gospel, "I am the bread of life. Whoever comes to me will never be hungry, and whoever believes in me will never be thirsty." Christians recognize the truth of this sacramental identity as they understand themselves to be receiving the life of Christ in the bread and wine of the Eucharist.

Once we've recognized what we call the "sacramental principle" in the person of Jesus, it becomes easier to see it working out all over the place. The God who we recognize in Jesus is disclosed in and through people, actions, and things that carry what we might call "added weight." For example, things such as water, fire, bread, wine, and oil may all carry added weight in particular situations. Or certain actions may do the same, such as washing, anointing, and breaking bread. The "things" and the "actions" are symbols of something greater than themselves, but even more than symbols, they may make God's presence and action so vividly alive and real to those encountering them in particular settings that they become sacramental. They become actual agents of change.

The Episcopal Church defines this sacramental principle like this: a sacrament is an "outward and visible sign of an inward and spiritual grace." So the outward sign of baptism is water, and the inward grace is union with Christ in his death and resurrection, the forgiveness of sins, and a new birth into God's family, the Church. The outward sign of Holy Communion is bread and wine. The inward grace is the Body and Blood of Christ.

I am the Bread of Life.

Pushing further still, it's clear that nature can take on a sacramental reality. "Earth's crammed with heaven, and every common bush afire with God," wrote Elizabeth Barrett Browning. "But only he who sees, takes off his shoes." In other words, it's the coming together of the person, action, or thing, with the recognition by the observer or participant, that causes the sacramental electricity to pass between them. That's when an object or action becomes sacramental.

For discussion

What might it mean that whoever comes to Christ will never be hungry?

Can you think of occasions when a person, an action, or a thing has taken on a sacramental meaning for you?

How could you develop a sense of the sacramental identity of ordinary things?

How many sacraments are there?

This could get controversial!

The two chief sacraments of the Church are Baptism and the Eucharist. They're called "dominical" sacraments because they are associated with the Lord himself (Latin *dominus*: lord, master). Baptism is the first step in a lifelong journey of discipleship, following Jesus day by day. The Eucharist is food for the journey and takes us closer to God.

However, Roman Catholics and some Episcoplains refer to five other sacraments: reconciliation, confirmation, marriage, ordination, and anointing of the sick. All of these can be channels of God's presence and action. In particular, many people have found that being anointed with oil when they have been ill has transformed their situation, whether in the spiritual resources they needed or in the actual state of their health. Similarly, the act of confession and absolution in the sacrament known as reconciliation has been found by many to be profoundly liberating, and many clergy lament the fact that the opportunity for such release is not taken up as often now as it used to be.

Two sacraments given us by Jesus himself and necessary for our Christian life—

- **Baptism**

- **Holy Communion**

Five sacramental rites of grace that have evolved in the Church under the guidance of the Holy Spirit—

- **Confirmation**—to make a mature commitment of faith

- **Reconciliation**—to assure us personally of God's forgiveness of our sins

- **Anointing of the sick**—to offer God's healing, strengthening, and transformation during times of illness and at life's end

- **Marriage**—for the joining together of two individuals in a lifelong covenant, the two becoming one flesh

- **Ordination**—the three historic orders of bishop, priest, and deacon that developed in the earliest days of the Church's life and ensure that continuity of ministry and service between the Church in this age and the Church in every age.

Confirmation is also sacramental. The is how The Episcopal Church defines it: "Confirmation is the rite in which we express a mature commitment to Christ, and receive strength from the Holy Spirit through prayer and the laying on of hands by a bishop."

Many of those who are discovering faith on the *Pilgrim* course will go on to Baptism and Confirmation, and then take their place around the table of the Lord. All that is required is a desire to know and receive Christ, penitence for our sins, and a readiness to confess him as Savior and obey him as Lord.

For discussion

- Returning to the stories we told each other at the beginning of the session about what worship means to us and the patterns we are developing, think about these other sacraments, the discipline of worship, and how the sacramental life shapes and sustains our discipleship. What else do you need to think about? What questions do you have of each other's stories?

- If you haven't been baptized or confirmed, is this something you need to think about?

- What questions do you have?

Journeying On

Go on thinking about how the whole of your life can become a hymn of praise and an offering to God, and how worship, through a pattern of daily prayer and Bible reading, and participation in the worship of the Church, can shape your life. You may also care to look at ordinary things and actions and see how they might be vehicles through which you can see the presence and action of God. Start developing a discipline of looking back at the day's events; go through them slowly and try to pick out the moments when God has been visible in the things you've seen and done and the people you've met.

Concluding Prayers

The cup of blessing that we bless,
is it not a sharing in the blood of Christ?
The bread that we break,
is it not a sharing in the body of Christ?
Because there is one bread,
we who are many are one body,
for we all partake of the one bread.

1 CORINTHIANS 10:16-17

Merciful God,
You have called us to your table.
Generous God,
You have fed us with the bread of life.
Abundant God,
Draw us and all people to the service of your Son;
And send us out to bring your peace and goodness to the world.
Amen.

Wisdom for the Journey

You see on God's altar bread and a cup. That is what the evidence of your eyes tells you but your faith requires you to believe that the bread is the body of Christ and the cup the blood of Christ. These things are called sacraments because our eyes see in them one thing and our understanding another. Our eyes see a material reality; our understanding perceives its spiritual effect. If you want to know what the body of Christ is, you must listen to what the apostle Paul tells the faithful: "Now you are the body of Christ, and individually you are members of it." If that is so, it is the sacrament of yourselves that is placed on the Lord's table, and it is the sacrament of yourselves that you are receiving. You reply "Amen" to what you are, and thereby agree that such you are. Be, then, a member of Christ's body, so that your "Amen" may accord with the truth.

AUGUSTINE (354–430)

Sacraments were instituted for the sake of sanctifying, as well as signifying.

PETER LOMBARD (1100–60)

As meat and drink do comfort the hungry body, so doth the death of Christ's body and the shedding of his blood comfort the soul, when she is after her sort hungry. There is no kind of meat that is comfortable to the soul, but only the death of Christ's blessed body; nor no kind of drink can quench her thirst, but only the blood-shedding of our Savior Christ, which was shed for her offenses.

THOMAS CRANMER (1489–1556)

Prayer the church's banquet, angel's age,
God's breath in man returning to his birth,
The soul in paraphrase, heart in pilgrimage,
The Christian plummet sounding heav'n and earth
Engine against th' Almighty, sinner's tow'r,
Reversed thunder, Christ-side-piercing spear,
The six-days world transposing in an hour,
A kind of tune, which all things hear and fear;
Softness, and peace, and joy, and love, and bliss,
Exalted manna, gladness of the best,
Heaven in ordinary, man well drest,
The milky way, the bird of Paradise,
Church-bells beyond the stars heard, the soul's blood,
The land of spices; something understood.

GEORGE HERBERT (1593–1633)

Our blessed savior has set us the brightest pattern of every virtue, and the best thing we can do is form ourselves upon this most perfect example.

MARY ASTELL (1668–1731)

NOTES

Introduction to *The Eucharist*
[1] John Donne (1572–1631), *Divine Poems: On the Sacrament.*
[2] Augustine (354–430), *Commentary on Psalm 41, 2.*

Opening Prayers for all sessions
Common Worship, Times and Seasons, London, Church House Publishing, 2006, p. 520 and Lucien Deiss, *Biblical Prayers*, Chicago, World Library Publications, 1976, p. 52.

Concluding Prayers for all sessions
Common Worship, Times and Seasons, London, Church House Publishing, 2006, p. 520 and *New Patterns for Worship*, London, Church House Publishing, 2002, p. 299 (adapted).

Session One
Justin (died *c.* 165), *First Apology.*
John Chrysostom (*c.* 347–407), *Homilies on St Matthew's Gospel*, 50, 4.
Bernard of Clairvaux (1090–1153), *On the Love of God*, 7.
J. S. B. Monsell (1811–75)
William Temple (1881–1944), *Christian Faith and Life*, London, SCM Press, 1931, p. 18.

Session Two
Justin (died *c.* 165), *First Apology.*
Hilary of Poitiers (315–67), *On the Trinity*, I.
Augustine (354–430), *Commentary on St John's Gospel*, 26, 13.
George Herbert (1593–1633), from "The Agonie."

Session Three
Irenaeus (130–*c.* 200), *Against the Heresies*, IV, 18.
Clement of Alexandria (150–215), *The Teacher*, 1.6.
Cyril of Jerusalem (*c.* 315–386), *Mystagogical Catecheses*, V, 21.
Gregory the Great (540–604), *Homily* 23.
George Herbert (1593–1633), *The Country Parson*, 22.
G. H. Bourne (1840–1925), "Lord Enthroned in Heavenly Splendour."
Anonymous (fourteenth century) *Anima Christi.*

Session Four
Anonymous, late first century, *Didache*, Ix, 4.
Augustine (354–430), *Sermon* 272.
Peter Chrysologus, fifth century.
Gregory the Great (540–604), *Homily* 23.

Session Five
Augustine (354–430), *Commentary on Psalm 41*, 2.
Evelyn Underhill (1875–1941), *Worship*, London, Nisbet & Co., 1936, p. 5.
Gregory Dix (1901–52), *The Shape of the Liturgy*, London, Dacre Press, 1945, p. 744.
Michael Ramsey (1904–88), *Be Still and Know: A Study in the Life of Prayer*, London, Collins, 1982, p. 123.

Session Six
Augustine (354–430), *Sermon* 272.
Peter Lombard (1100–60), *Sentences*, IV, 1.
Thomas Cranmer (1489–1556), *A Defense of the True and Catholic Doctrine of the Sacrament of the Body and Blood of our Savior Christ.*
George Herbert (1593–1633), "Prayer."
Mary Astell (1668–1731), *The Christian Religion as Profess'd by a Daughter of the Church of England*, London, 1705, p. 158.